W9-AYM-940

ROBOTS AND ROBOTICS

MANUFACTURING ROBOTS

DANIEL R. FAUST

PowerKiDS press™

New York

Published in 2017 by The Rosen Publishing Group, Inc.
29 East 21st Street, New York, NY 10010

First Edition

Editor: Caitie McAneney
Book Design: Reann Nye

Photo Credits: Cover, p. 11 Praphan Jampala/Shutterstock.com; p. 4 https://commons.wikimedia.org/wiki/File:Capek_play.jpg; pp. 5, 17, 21 (delta robot, articulated robot) asharkyu/Shutterstock.com; p. 7 Tatiana Popova/Shutterstock.com; p. 8 https://commons.wikimedia.org/wiki/File:Shakey.png; p. 9 Andrei Kholmov/Shutterstock.com; p. 12 wi6995/Shutterstock.com; pp. 13, 30 Baloncici/Shutterstock.com; p. 15 Nataliya Hora /Shutterstock.com; p. 18 http://commons.wikimedia.org/wiki/File:TOSY_Parallel_Robot.JPG; p. 19 Dario Sabljak/Shutterstock.com; p. 21 (gantry robot) Leonid Shtishevskiy/Shutterstock.com; p. 21 (SCARA robot) https://commons.wikimedia.org/wiki/File:SCARA_mit_Stocker.jpg;p. 22 Hulton Collection/Hulton Archive/Getty Images; p. 23 bibiphoto/Shutterstock.com;p. 24 BORIS HORVAT/AFP/Getty Images; p. 25 Bloomberg/Getty Images; p. 27 michaeljung/Shutterstock.com; p. 28 Javier Larrea/age fotostock/Getty Images; p. 29 ndoeljindoel/Shutterstock.com.

Cataloging-in-Publication Data

Names: Faust, Daniel R.
Title: Manufacturing robots / Daniel R. Faust
Description: New York : PowerKids Press, 2017. | Series: Robots and robotics | Includes index.
Identifiers: ISBN 9781499421712 (pbk.) | ISBN 9781499421736 (library bound) | ISBN 9781499421729 (6 pack)
Subjects: LCSH: Robots–Juvenile literature. | Robots, Industrial–Juvenile literature.
Classification: LCC TJ211.2 F38 2017| DDC 629.8'92–dc23

Manufactured in the United States of America

CPSIA Compliance Information: Batch #BS16PK: For Further Information contact Rosen Publishing, New York, New York at 1-800-237-9932

CONTENTS

WHAT IS A ROBOT?

In 1920, Czech writer Karel Čapek published a science-fiction play called *R.U.R.: Rossum's Universal Robots*. Čapek's play was about a factory that makes **artificial** humans known as robots. The word came from the Czech word "robota," which means "forced labor." This was the first time that the word "robot" was used. Although the robots in Čapek's play were living things, the term was soon applied to mechanical devices.

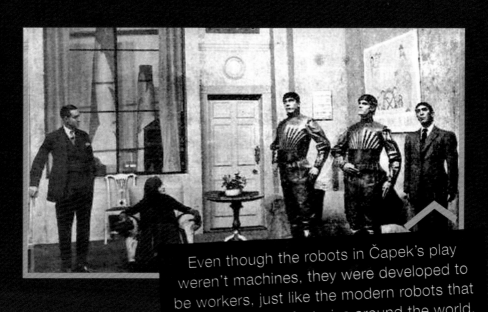

Even though the robots in Čapek's play weren't machines, they were developed to be workers, just like the modern robots that currently work in factories around the world.

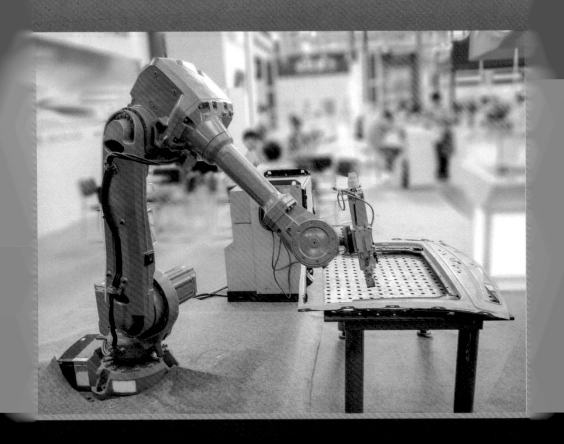

Like the robots in Čapek's play, many modern robots
ere designed to be workers. A robot worker is the perfec
swer for a job that's too dangerous, or unsafe, for a
man worker. Robots can be programmed to perform
e same job over and over for hours at a time, which is
mething that even the best human worker might not be

ROBOTS AT THE FACTORY

Robots have actually been around for a lot longer than you might think. The earliest robots were mechanical devices called automata. From the 1600s to the 1800s, automata were built to entertain and amuse members of the highest classes of Europe.

One of the first automata invented for manufacturing was an automated **loom**, which was built in 1750 by French inventor Jacques de Vaucanson. His loom made him little money, but he became known for making automata that played instruments. About 50 years later, a French weaver named Joseph Marie Jacquard perfected a way to control an automated loom. The loom was programmed using a chain of punch cards. Each hole controlled a hook on the loom. This allowed the loom to produce different patterns.

This timeline shows important events in the development of robots. Each early robot advanced the field and, in some way, inspired the **complex** manufacturing robots we have today.

TIMELINE OF ROBOTICS

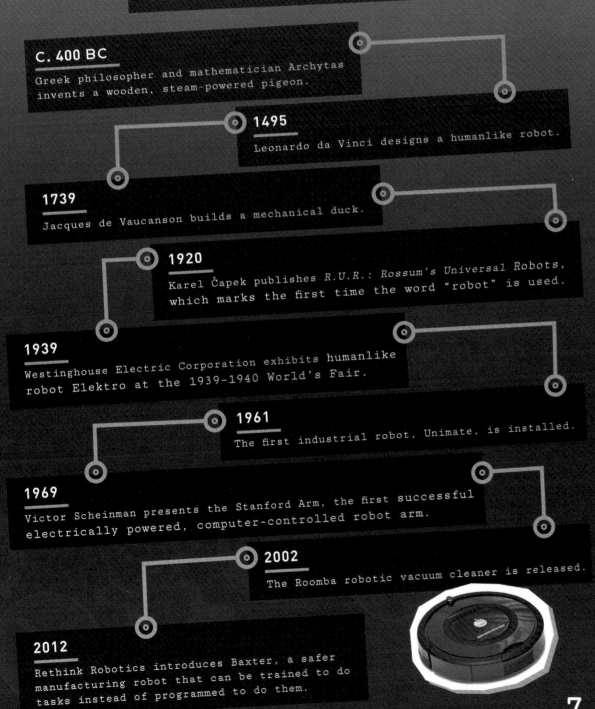

C. 400 BC
Greek philosopher and mathematician Archytas invents a wooden, steam-powered pigeon.

1495
Leonardo da Vinci designs a humanlike robot.

1739
Jacques de Vaucanson builds a mechanical duck.

1920
Karel Čapek publishes *R.U.R.: Rossum's Universal Robots*, which marks the first time the word "robot" is used.

1939
Westinghouse Electric Corporation exhibits humanlike robot Elektro at the 1939–1940 World's Fair.

1961
The first industrial robot, Unimate, is installed.

1969
Victor Scheinman presents the Stanford Arm, the first successful electrically powered, computer-controlled robot arm.

2002
The Roomba robotic vacuum cleaner is released.

2012
Rethink Robotics introduces Baxter, a safer manufacturing robot that can be trained to do tasks instead of programmed to do them.

The end of the 20th century saw big steps in computers and computer programming. This growth built upon the work of earlier inventors and mathematicians, such as Charles Babbage, Ada Lovelace, and Alan Turing. Their work paved the way for robots that could be programmed to do certain tasks. The manufacturing world would be changed forever.

MEET SHAKEY!

Shakey was the first robot able to sense its environment and make decisions based on its surroundings. SRI International's Artificial Intelligence Center developed Shakey between 1966 and 1972. Shakey was able to plan and perform tasks, such as rearranging objects. Shakey greatly influenced the fields of computer programming and robotics. It was so popular that *Life* magazine called it the "first electronic person." Today, you can visit Shakey at the Computer History Museum in Mountain View, California.

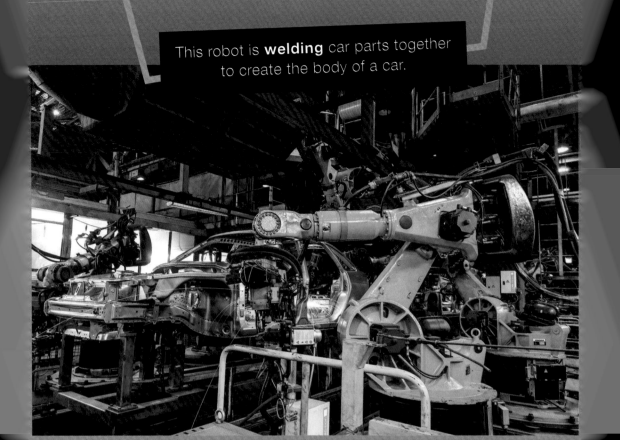

This robot is **welding** car parts together to create the body of a car.

In 1954, American inventor George Devol Jr. designed the first programmable robot. Two years later, Devol teamed up with American engineer Joseph Engelberger to form the first robotics company—Unimation. In 1961, Devol and Engelberger introduced the Unimate. The Unimate was a robotic arm designed to perform **repetitive** or dangerous jobs on an **assembly line**. The Unimate was the first robot

PARTS OF A ROBOT

You use different parts of your body to interact with your environment in different ways. Your eyes and ears tell you about the world around you. You use your legs to run, jump, and dance. Your arms and hands let you reach out and pick something up. And your brain controls it all. You might be surprised to learn this, but robots are a lot like you. A robot has different parts to perform different tasks.

A robot's sensors are like your eyes and ears. They gather information about the robot's surroundings and help guide its movement. Most robots have simple motion detectors that alert them when they're about to hit an **obstacle**, but some robots have advanced cameras and microphones that work just as well as your eyes and ears.

This huge overhead robot needs sensors to know the location of the product it's working on and if an obstacle is in its way.

11

This manufacturing robot uses welding guns to perform its job. The welding guns are its effectors.

A robot's moving components, or parts, are called effectors and actuators. Effectors are components that allow robots to perform specific physical tasks, such as picking up and moving objects. They're like the robot's arms and hands.

Actuators are the motors that make the effectors move. They also provide power to the wheels, treads, and propellers that help the robot move from one place to another. Many manufacturing robots stand still, but

The controller is the final basic component. The controller is a computer that acts as the robot's brain. It takes the information gathered from the robot's sensors and decides the best way for the robot to move and interact with the environment to complete a given task.

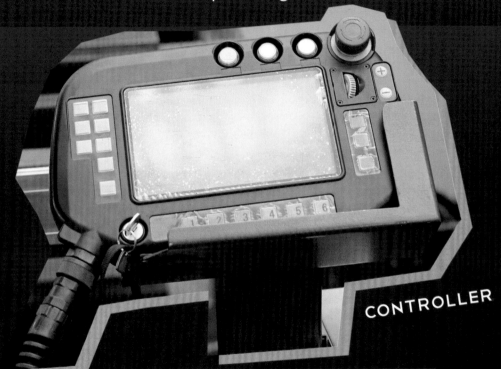

CONTROLLER

END EFFECTORS

End effectors are the tools attached to the end of a robot's arm that allow the robot to complete the tasks it's programmed to perform. The form and function of the end effector depends on the job the robot is expected to do. A robot can be fitted with different kinds of end effectors. Common end effectors include grippers, cutting tools, drills, magnets, spray guns, and welding guns. What tasks do you think each of these effectors could complete?

ARTICULATED ROBOTS

When you think about manufacturing robots, you probably picture large robotic arms working on a factory assembly line. These kinds of manufacturing robots are often articulated robots. The word "articulated" means something has two or more sections connected by a flexible joint. Articulated robots are robots that have one or more **rotary** joints, allowing their components to move around.

Although robots can have articulated legs, it's more common to see articulated robots built to resemble arms. Articulated robots are used in factories to cut and weld. Police departments and the military use robots equipped with articulated arms to handle explosives and other dangerous materials. The *Phoenix* Mars lander used by the National Aeronautics and Space Administration (NASA) was also equipped with articulated robot arms to perform

Articulated robots are what most people think of when they imagine manufacturing robots. Their joints give them a wide range of movement, making them productive workers.

Selective Compliance Assembly Robotic Arm (SCARA) robots are similar to articulated robots in many ways. Like articulated robots, SCARA robots function a lot like the human arm. The main difference between the two types of robots is the mobility of the robot's "wrist." Unlike articulated robots, SCARA robots have wrist joints that can rotate around, but can't tilt up and down.

SCARA robots are known for their speed and **precision**, as well as their ability to be used for multiple tasks. These robots are used primarily for material-handling or "pick-and-place" operations. SCARA robots can move materials quickly and efficiently, making them perfect for both assembly work and packaging. These types of robots can even be waterproofed to work in underwater construction.

SCARA robots are used in many factories because they work quickly and they are some of the most affordable manufacturing robots.

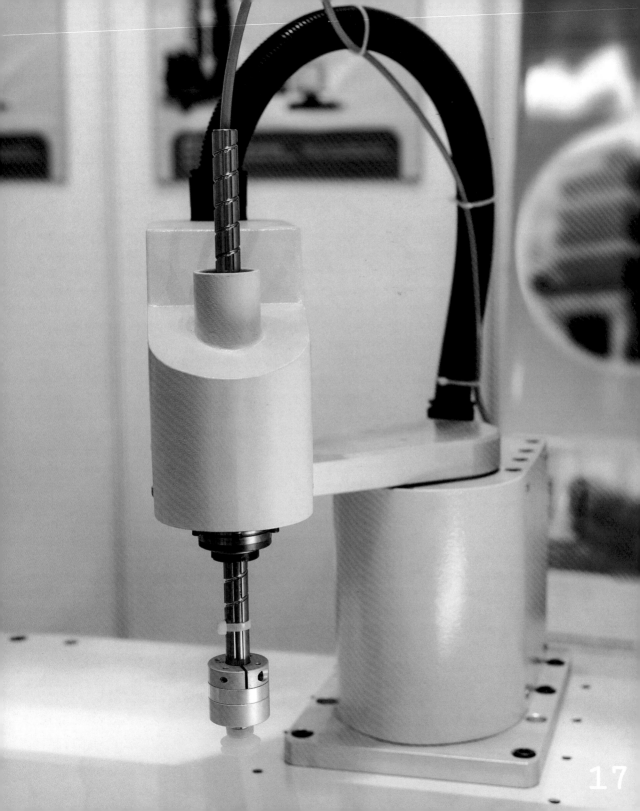

DELTA ROBOTS

Delta robots are a type of parallel robot. Parallel [robots] use multiple arms working together to control [an] effector. In the case of a delta robot, three arms [work] to move and control its effector. The delta robot [was in-]vented in the early 1980s to quickly **manipulate** light objects. At a time when the components of [many] things, such as electronics, were getting smalle[r, the delta] robot became increasingly popular.

Delta robots are used in a number of industries, including the packaging, electronics, and medical industries. Their ability to manipulate items with speed and precision makes delta robots perfect for pick-and-place tasks. Recently, delta robots have become key components in some 3-D printers.

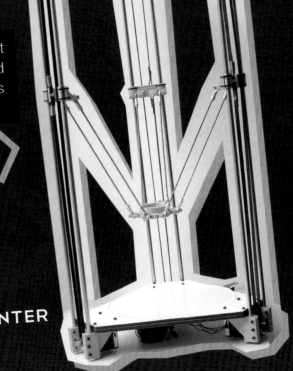

The multiple arms of the delta robot are connected to a single base and a single effector. This delta robot is part of a 3-D printer.

3-D PRINTER

Gantry robots are used in many different industries, from car manufacturing to medicine manufacturing. They can only move in straight lines, up and down and side to side.

A gantry robot has a manipulator arm mounted onto an overhead system that allows it to work from above in large open spaces, such as warehouses and factories. These robots are also useful in situations where floor space is limited. Gantry robots are perfect for pick-and-place tasks, but they can also be used for operations such as welding and drilling. They're often used to move items around warehouses and other spaces that may be too crowded for floor-mounted robots. They're easy to program and prized for their precision.

CHOOSE YOUR ROBOT

ARTICULATED ROBOT
- one or more rotary joints
- wide range of movement

SCARA ROBOT
- wrist joints can rotate but not tilt
- less mobile than articulated robots

DELTA ROBOT
- parallel robot, has multiple arms and single effector
- good for small, light objects

GANTRY ROBOT
- moves only in straight lines
- manipulator arm on overhead system

The different types of robots have different strengths and weaknesses. Companies have to choose the best robot for their tasks.

THE ASSEMBLY LINE

1913, Henry Ford started the first moving
bile assembly line in his factory in Detroit, Mic
e allowed workers, each assigned a specific ta
mble an automobile in six hours. Before that, t
mally took 12 and a half hours. Over 100 year
e moving assembly line is still a key compone
cturing around the world.

Ford's assembly line greatly impro
production and made his business

Of course, today's assembly line is a little different. In modern factories, people work side by side with manufacturing robots. Large factories use articulated robots, SCARA robots, delta robots, and gantry robots. They perform different tasks quickly, efficiently, and safely. Robots are used to cut and place **fabricated** parts, assemble machinery, paint, weld, drill, fasten, measure

IN THE WAREHOUSE

Robots aren't only used to manufacture goods. They're also used in the warehouses that store and deliver those goods. Robots can be used to move products around a warehouse, from the loading docks to packing and shipping areas. Robots are also used to stack goods on shipping pallets. Some warehouses have robots that can move shelves closer to their human coworkers, making sure more popular items are easier to find. Companies like the online store Amazon are even looking at ways to use flying robots to ship products from their warehouses directly to customers.

These orange robots by Kiva Systems are used in warehouses to greatly improve productivity. Not only can they bring entire shelves of products to human workers, but they can also adjust the placement of shelves based on the popularity of items.

Many companies depend on robot technology, but robots haven't completely replaced human workers. Robots lack the ability to **improvise** and operate outside

INSPECTIONS AND QUALITY CONTROL

Inspections and quality control are two important parts of the manufacturing industry. Routine inspections of factories and factory equipment make sure they're safe for human workers. Quality control makes sure the products a factory makes meet customers' expectations.

Companies have begun using robots for inspections, which used to be a strictly human job. A robot arm equipped with a camera can be used to inspect dangerous factory equipment. Robots can test the same products over and over and make sure they're all the same. Robots also have greater strength to test large products, such as huge airplane parts. Some robots are small enough to inspect tight spaces in a factory. They can also be used to handle dangerous materials needed for some industries, such as the chemical manufacturing industry.

These workers are inspecting factory equipment to make sure it's working correctly. In the future, robots may take over many inspection jobs.

ROBOT COWORKERS

Ever since the first robot was used on an automobile assembly line, people have been concerned that robots will one day replace human workers completely. However, while one industrial robot can do the job of several human workers, human employees are still needed. In fact, the next generation of industrial robots is being designed to work alongside human employees.

THE THREE LAWS OF ROBOTICS

In 1942, author Isaac Asimov published a short story titled "Runaround." In this story, Asimov created the Three Laws of Robotics. Asimov's laws for robot behavior have frequently been used as a guideline for how robots and humans should interact. The first law states that a robot may not injure a human being or allow them to be harmed. The second law declares that a robot has to obey human orders, except when they may harm someone. The final law states a robot must protect itself, as long as that doesn't cause it to break either of the first two laws.

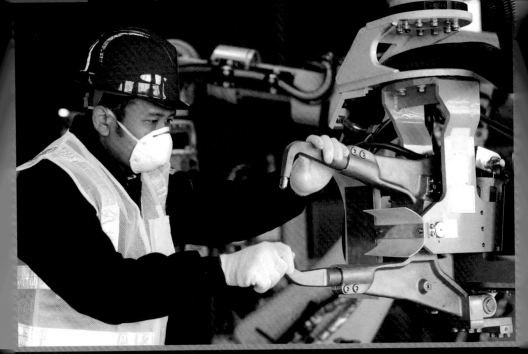

Researchers and inventors are working on ways to make industrial robots more **collaborative**. They're finding ways that robots and humans can work together. The biggest challenge to this is worker safety. Older industrial robots could easily injure a person with their large steel arms. Newer robots use cameras and other technology to sense where people are and change direction or stop to

THE FUTURE OF MANUFACTURING

What will the factories of tomorrow look like? Will the warehouses of the future have any human employees? Some people think the future will be completely automated, with robots taking over every job once held by humans. It might be cool to imagine a future where smart factories and smart warehouses are staffed and operated entirely by robot workers, but it isn't likely to happen.

As robots become smaller and cheaper, more companies will be able to add robot workers. Even a small company would be able to add robots to its human workforce, which would increase the company's productivity and profits. It's more likely that the workplace of tomorrow will be a collaborative workplace where robots and humans work together.

GLOSSARY

artificial: Made by people and not by nature.

assembly line: An arrangement of machines, equipment, and workers in which work passes down the line until the product is assembled.

collaborative: Involving people or groups working together.

complex: Having to do with something with many parts that work together.

fabricated: Made or constructed.

improvise: To make, invent, or arrange on short notice.

loom: A hand-operated or power-driven device for weaving fabrics.

manipulate: To move or control something.

obstacle: Something that makes it difficult to complete an action.

precision: The quality of being exact or accurate.

repetitive: Happening again and again.

rotary: Able to turn around a central point like a wheel.

weld: To join two pieces of metal together by melting them

INDEX

WEBSITES

Due to the changing nature of Internet links, PowerKids Press has developed an online list of websites related to the subject of this book. This site is updated regularly. Please use this link to access the list: www.powerkidslinks.com/rar/manu